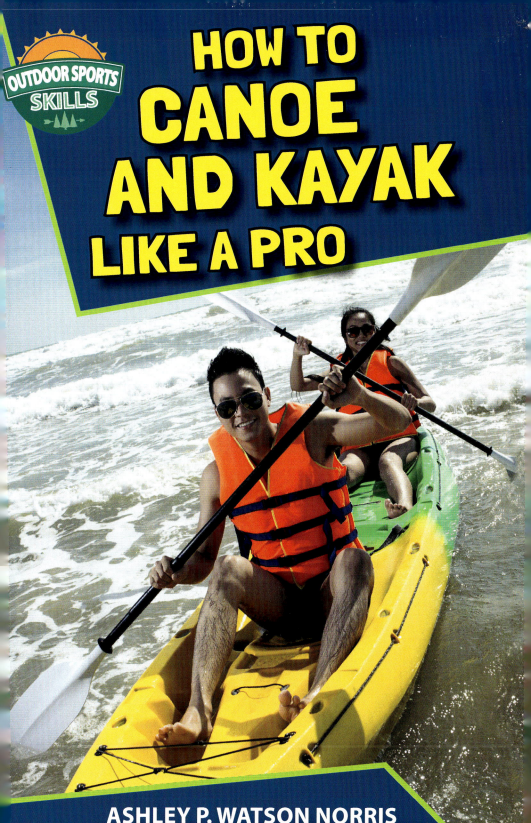

Outdoor Sports Skills

HOW TO CANOE AND KAYAK
LIKE A PRO

ASHLEY P. WATSON NORRIS

Library of Congress Cataloging-in-Publication Data

Norris, Ashley P. Watson.
  How to canoe and kayak like a pro / Ashley P. Watson Norris.
    pages cm. — (Outdoor sports skills)
  Includes bibliographical references and index.
  Summary: "In this 'How-to' guide, learn the basic skills of canoeing and kayaking including how to
    launch a canoe and kayak, how to read a river, and how to stay safe while out on the water"—
    Provided by publisher.
  ISBN 978-1-62285-244-4
  1. Canoes and canoeing—Juvenile literature. 2. Kayaking—Juvenile literature. I. Title.
GV784.3.N67 2014
797.122—dc23
              2013040826
Future editions:
Paperback ISBN: 978-1-62285-245-1   Single-User PDF ISBN: 978-1-62285-247-5
EPUB ISBN: 978-1-62285-246-8   Multi-User PDF ISBN: 978-1-62285-248-2

Printed in the United States of America
062014 The HF Group, North Manchester, IN
10 9 8 7 6 5 4 3 2 1

To Our Readers: We have done our best to make sure all Internet addresses in this book were active
and appropriate when we went to press. However, the author and the publisher have no control over
and assume no liability for the material available on those Internet sites or on other Web sites they may
link to. Any comments or suggestions can be sent by e-mail to comments@speedingstar.com or to the
address below:

Speeding Star

Speeding Star
Box 398, 40 Industrial Road
Berkeley Heights, NJ 07922
USA
www.speedingstar.com

Enslow Publishers, Inc., is committed to printing our books on recycled paper. The paper in every
book contains 10% to 30% post-consumer waste (PCW). The cover board on the outside of each book
contains 100% PCW. Our goal is to do our part to help young people and the environment too!

Illustration Credits: Shutterstock: (©maratr, p. 5; ©Dr. Morley Read, p. 6; © Ivan Smuk, p. 8; © Jim David,
pp. 10(top), 36; ©Ivan Chudakov, p. 10(bottom); ©bikeriderlondon, p. 13; ©MountainHardcore, p. 14;
©Pavel L Photo and Video, p. 15; © travis manley, p. 17; ©Ariwasabi, p. 19; ©Venus Angel, p. 20; ©Elena
Elisseeva, p. 22; ©falk, p. 27; ©Oleg Zabielin, p. 30; ©James Wheeler, p. 31; ©mikeledray, p. 32; ©Tracing
Tea, p. 33; © Dmitry Naumov, p. 35; © LesPalenik, pp. 37, 43; ©Strahil Dimitrov, 39; ©John Kropewnicki,
p. 41; ©Vince Clements, p. 42; ©Pecold, p. 45) ©Thinkstock: (JupiterimagesCollection/Stockbyte, pp.
4, 29; RJAPHOTOCollection/iStock, p. 7; Stockbyte, p. 21; Ron Chapple StockCollectionRon Chapple
Studios, p. 25.

Cover Illustration: ©Thinkstock/DragonImagesCollection/iStock

CONTENTS

FUNDAMENTALS

EXPLORING WATERWAYS

Canoes and kayaks open up a new, exciting world along the water's edge. They allow paddlers to go where cars, bicycles, motorboats, hikers, and swimmers cannot. These small watercraft can silently slip along the banks of rivers, lakes, and oceans. They can maneuver up small streams and creeks that large boats cannot navigate.

Gliding swiftly and silently over the water in a canoe or kayak gives complete freedom and control to the paddler. They control their speed and decide on their destination. A paddler can find privacy and study nature up close in quiet river waters or answer the challenge of a fast-moving white-water rapid.

By packing in a smart way, canoes and kayaks can be used for an all-day outing or for several days of camping. Canoes can

Using a canoe or kayak makes exploring smaller bodies of water like creeks or river banks possible.

4

With a kayak, these young women are exploring.

be large enough to hold several people, and sufficient fodd and supplies.

Because canoes and kayaks are small human-powered watercraft, they are quiet, giving the chance to see wildlife up close and undisturbed. Remember to pack binoculars and a guidebook to identify plants and wildlife. Many will see animals drinking at the water's edge, such as foxes, deer, moose, or even wolves!

Paddlers can go alone or bring their best friend, whether that is a human or a dog. The possibilities are endless.

WHAT IS CANOEING?

Canoes are the pickup trucks of the boating world. They can carry lots of gear and a few passengers. They sit high on the water and provide good visibility. Canoes are more stable and easier to get into and out of than a kayak. They're best suited for calm water, but with the right equipment can go into rough water.

The very first canoes were logs that were paddled by hand or with poles pushed off the bottom of a riverbed. They evolved into hollowed-out trees, and then wooden or bone frames with animal skins stretched over them.

When Christopher Columbus landed in the New World he reported that the native Arawak Indians used hollowed-out tree trunks to navigate the sea. Columbus called

People in some parts of the world still use canoes as simple and basic as the first canoes.

them *kenus*. That is where the modern word, canoe, originates. American Indians have used various types of handmade canoes for thousands of years from readily available materials.

Modern recreational canoes are made from plastic, fiberglass, Kevlar, and aluminum. They have open tops, have pointed ends, and are long, light, and narrow. They usually fit several people sitting or kneeling. The paddler, or paddlers, face the direction of travel and use a single-bladed paddle to propel the canoe forward.

For a quiet and patient canoer or kayaker, seeing some of nature's beautiful scenery is one of the many great things that can be experienced while out exploring on the water. This young woman is kayaking in the Everglades.

Canoers can either sit or kneel. Sitting in a canoe is similar to sitting on a bench. The paddler sits on the seat with his or her legs bent at the knee. Many canoers kneel because it lowers their center of gravity, which makes the canoe more stable.

WHAT IS KAYAKING?

Kayaks are the rugged, off-road cars of the boating world. They are narrower and shallower than canoes. Kayaks have less cargo capacity than canoes, and are

Canoes come in various sizes. Some are built larger and with more seats to accommodate additional riders.

more maneuverable and faster in the water. Their sit-inside design allows kayaks to go over rougher water than canoes and not swamp, or fill with water.

Kayaks were invented by the Inuit who lived in the Arctic and sub-Arctic areas of Alaska, Canada, Greenland, and northeast Russia. They have been in use for thousands of years to hunt and fish in the summer when the water is not frozen.

Inuits used bones and wood covered by animal skins to build their kayaks. They used boiled animal fat to keep the skin waterproof. Their paddles had blades at both ends to give them more control and power when navigating though rough waters.

Inuits, formerly called Eskimos, wore a seal-skin jacket called a tuilik that they laced to the kayak. If the kayak flipped over in rough, ice-cold water the tuiliks kept them relatively dry while they flipped their kayak right-side up again. This movement is still called an Eskimo roll.

Modern kayaks hold one or two people. Kayakers sit on a seat on the floor of the kayak with their legs extended in front of them. There are many different styles of kayaks. Most cover the paddler's legs. Recreational sit-on-top kayaks are the exception.

FITNESS & SKILLS

Paddling does not require extreme fitness, but being fit will make paddling even more fun. It will allow for longer trips and decrease the chances of getting injured. Beginning paddlers should start with short trips to build strength, skills, and make exercising part

DID YOU KNOW?

The word kayak means hunter's boat.

Most people start off learning to kayak in calmer waters before going after the rougher and more dangerous white water.

of a daily routine. As fitness increases, and water skills are developed paddlers can safely work their way up to longer, more difficult trips.

Out-of-the-water training is important to provide full-body fitness. That means more strength, power, and endurance when paddling. Running and cycling are good ways to increase leg strength. Sit-ups and crunches will build strong abdominal muscles.

A good full-body workout is swimming. Plus, it is a crucial safety skill. Every paddler needs to know how to swim. If a boat flips, paddlers must be able to swim from the boat to shore.

Tying knots is an important boating skill. A good knot is easy to tie, untie, and secures a rope to an object, a rope to another rope, or locks down gear.

Two important knots to know are the bowline and the sheet bend knot. The bowline knot forms a loop at the end of a rope that will not slip. It is great for attaching a boat's towline to a tree. The sheet bend knot makes it possible to tie two ropes together. Practice with some extra rope or string until it becomes second nature.

GEAR

CANOES

Some common boating terms that are good to know and will impress friends:

Bow—[pronounced bou] front of the boat
Stern—back of the boat
Port—left side
Starboard—right side
Hull—the main body of the canoe
Gunwale—top rail around the outside of the canoe
Thwart—support braces that help the canoe keep its shape
Rocker—the upward curve at the stern and bow

Canoes are designed for specific uses. Their use will determine the shape of the hull, bottom, length, and rocker. The more rocker a canoe has, the easier the canoe is to turn.

Recreational canoes have wide, flat bottoms that make them stable and slow.

Touring canoes are made to carry people and gear far. Their hulls are longer, they can hold lots of gear, they're faster, and have a shallow arched hull.

White-water canoes are made to move quickly so they are short, have rounded hulls, and lots of rocker to get around rocks and rough rapids.

Racing canoes are designed to be smaller so that they can quickly glide through the water.

PRO TIPS AND TRICKS

If more than one person is inside the canoe, the more experienced canoer should sit in the back. Being in the back of the canoe is better for controlling which direction the canoe is going.

Racing canoes are made to be fast and go in a straight line. They are long, narrow, have a shallow V-shaped hull, and little rocker.

The most popular materials used to build canoes are plastic, fiberglass, Kevlar, and wood. Plastic is very durable, does not require much maintenance, is the least expensive, but is heavy. Fiberglass canoes vary in weight and costs. They are strong and easily repaired. Kevlar is very lightweight and strong but is expensive, hard to maintain, and difficult to repair.

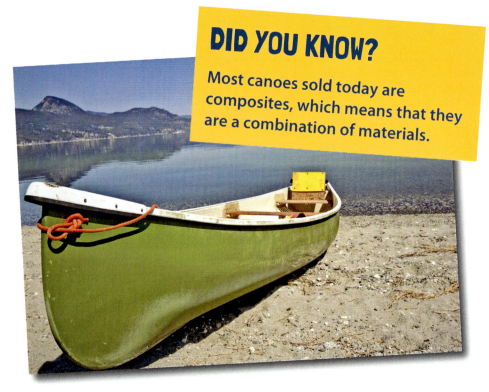

DID YOU KNOW?

Most canoes sold today are composites, which means that they are a combination of materials.

One of the benefits of using a fiberglass canoe is that they are much more durable and have a longer life than wood or metal canoes.

PRO TIPS AND TRICKS

The "Law of Gross Tonnage" is a unwritten rule when it comes to boating that should be applied to the canoeing and kayaking world. To put it short, it means that when on the water, the bigger boat will win. Big boats have a harder time slowing down and turning, so the responsibility to avoid contact with bigger boats is on canoers and kayakers.

When kayakers are shown next to a yacht, it becomes clear why the Law of Gross Tonnage works against kayakers and canoers.

KAYAKS

Boating terminology is used with kayaks also but there are a few other words to know:

Deck—top of the kayak
Hull—bottom of the kayak
Cockpit—the area where the paddler sits
Hatch—opening to an inside compartment of the
    kayak used for storage
Coaming—the outside edge of the cockpit

The front and rear deck have bungee cords stretched across them to hold items down. At the stern is the rudder that helps control the direction of the kayak. It is controlled by foot pedals inside the cockpit.

Recreational kayaks are the most popular and designed with a wide flat bottom to make it stable, and easy to get in and out of. They are great for beginners.

Sea and touring kayaks are long, narrow, and have little rocker because they are meant to go for long distances in a straight line. They are heavy and have a rounded hull that can carry lots of supplies.

White-water kayaks are the sports cars of the kayak world. They are fast, sleek-looking, and agile. They are short, have no storage room, rounded hulls, and lots of rocker to maneuver.

Sport kayaks are designed for the specific sport. Fishing kayaks will have places to put rods and coolers. Scuba kayaks will be designed to hold tanks. Surf kayaks are similar to white-water kayaks but made to surf in the ocean.

Sit-on-top kayaks do not cover the paddler's legs and are difficult to flip. They are easy to get in and out of but offer no protection for the paddler.

PADDLES

Canoe paddles have only one blade and a grip at the opposite end. Kayak paddles have a blade at both ends. Other than that, the basics of a paddle are the same. Paddles have a shaft, throat, blade, and tip.

The blade has two faces; the powerface and the backface. The powerface is seen by the paddler, and the backface faces away from the paddler.

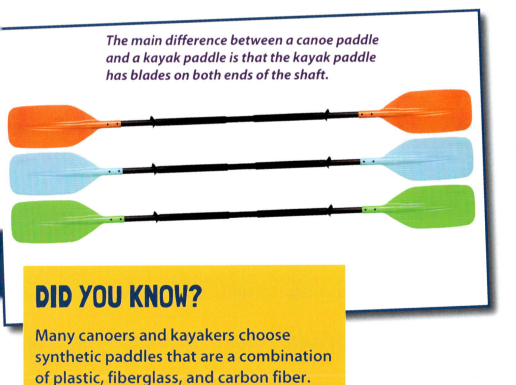

The main difference between a canoe paddle and a kayak paddle is that the kayak paddle has blades on both ends of the shaft.

DID YOU KNOW?

Many canoers and kayakers choose synthetic paddles that are a combination of plastic, fiberglass, and carbon fiber.

Choosing the right size paddle is paramount. To size a canoe paddle, pretend to be in a canoe and get in the same paddling position. Put the grip on the floor. The paddle throat should be about nose level.

Recreational kayak paddles are sized by standing height. An average adult uses a 220-cm (86-inch) paddle. Shorter adults and children should choose a smaller paddle that fits them.

Once the correct size is found, practice paddling the air. Pick one with a shaft that feels comfortable. The smaller the blade and lighter the paddle, the easier it will be to paddle. Wooden canoe paddles are classics, but they can be heavy.

Hold a canoe paddle with one hand on the grip and the other on the throat. Have a relaxed grip a little wider than shoulder width. Hold a kayak paddle in a loose grip with hands shoulder width apart.

GEAR & CLOTHES

Always, always, always plan on getting wet!

If it is cold, dress in layers of wool or synthetic fabrics that dry quickly or are water repellent to keep warm. In extremely cold weather wear a wet suit to keep warm. Keep ears warm with a fleece beanie.

PRO TIPS AND TRICKS

Do not wear cotton in cold weather. The phrase, "cotton kills" is true. It takes a long time to dry and as it dries cotton actually makes the wearer colder.

On a sunny and warm day the best clothing may be a bathing suit. Wear sunglasses to protect eyes from the sun and its glare off the water. Remember to put on sunscreen and wear a wide-brimmed hat.

A helmet is standard head gear for white-water paddlers. It protects their head as they bounce around in the rapids.

Spray skirts are optional for sit-inside kayaks. They prevent water from entering the cockpit. They create a seal around the paddler at the waist and around the kayak at the cockpit coaming.

This kayaker is well-prepared for a trip on a glacier lake in Norway. She wears warm clothing, headgear to keep her ears and head warm, and sunglasses.

Anything that should not get wet should be kept in a waterproof bag, called a dry bag. They come in many sizes, shapes, and colors. Dry bags can be large enough to hold a sleeping bag. Small, clear voice-through dry bags are available for cell phones.

Transporting a canoe or kayak from the garage to the water requires a car top carrier or a boat trailer. Kayaks are easily strapped sideways on top of a car. Canoes should be placed upside down on top of a car. Then proper ropes should be used to secure the vessel in the middle, at the bow, and at the stern.

A dry bag is important to have with you to keep everything from getting wet, like a cell phones and car keys.

TRANSPORTING A CANOE

Carrying canoes and kayaks is a lot easier with two people. One person holds the bow and the other holds the stern. They either carry it on its side or lift it over their heads and flip it upside down. When carrying a canoe or kayak be careful not to hit anyone or anything!

The toughest part about only one person carrying a kayak or a coanoe is trying to set it down without dropping it.

Getting into a canoe can be tricky, but by getting in with part of the canoe on land makes it easier. Then the canoers can just push off using their paddles.

PRO TIPS AND TRICKS

Avoid standing, turning around quickly, or reaching and leaning outside the canoe to reduce the chance of having the canoe capsize. Any movement inside the canoe should be done slow and steady.

A one-person carry is easy with a cart or trolley, however they are not necessary. The easiest one-person carry is the suitcase carry. Go to the middle of the canoe, squat down, roll the canoe of its side, put the gunwale on a shoulder and stand up. At the water's edge, do not slam the canoe down, carefully place it on the ground.

Getting into a canoe is trickier than it looks! Falling into the water happens a lot. Make sure to put on a life jacket before getting in. Also, make sure the paddle is in the boat and not floating away or on shore.

Place the canoe parallel to the shore or dock. Make sure the canoe is deep enough so it will not get stuck on the bottom after all the paddlers and gear are loaded.

Solo paddlers hold onto the sides, or gunwale, to keep a low center of gravity and step gently into the center of the canoe one foot at a time. Tandem paddlers should have one person steady the canoe while the other enters and gets settled. The first paddler to enter should keep as low a center of gravity as possible to help stabilize the canoe as the second paddler gets in.

LAUNCHING A KAYAK

Before getting in a kayak make sure to put on a life jacket. Keep a good solid hold on the paddle or attach it to the kayak's bungee cords so it will not float away.

To get into a kayak from the beach, have the kayak face the direction of travel. Straddle the kayak and walk toward the cockpit. Sit down in the seat and one at a time, slowly place feet into the cockpit. For tandem kayakers one person should steady the boat while the other person gets in. Then the person in the kayak needs to keep still while the second person climbs inside.

Once seated, sit up straight and place feet on the footrests. Kayaks with rudders will have rudder pedals that are adjustable. Legs should be slightly bent and knees pressed outward against the hull. This leg position will help maintain balance and control in choppy water. To control the rudder push down with the toe of the foot in the direction of travel.

To attach a spray skirt, grab the back of the skirt and tuck it around the back cockpit coaming. Slowly work the spray skirt around the entire cockpit. Make sure that the release strap on the front of the spray skirt is sticking out. If the kayak flips, grab the release strap and pull out and up. Practice this in shallow water several times until it becomes second nature.

HOW TO STEER & PADDLE

Hand paddled boats always weave back and forth. It is the paddler's challenge to keep as straight a line as possible by using the rudder and paddling techniques.

Paddling is an art and it requires many different muscles. It takes time and practice to do the forward stroke well. It is the most important stroke to know because it is used the most. Arms are used to guide

Because a kayak uses a paddle with blades on each side of the shaft, the paddling motion is different from that of a canoe.

the paddle while the larger muscles of the abdomen, shoulders, and back provide power to the stroke.

Canoers keep a hand on the grip in front of them around face height. This hand will not move much but will help rotate the face of the paddle. Plant the blade into the water but not to the throat. Now rotate the torso and use the abdominal muscles to propel the canoe forward. The forward stroke is short and from where the blade is planted to where it is withdrawn from the water is less than two feet long.

Kayakers rotate at the hips and extend one arm forward then plant the blade up to the throat in the water. Then straighten the hips while relaxing the top hand and push forward. The top hand comes across the body. Remove the blade from the water when it gets to the hips. This position sets the paddler up to do a stroke with the opposite blade the exact same way.

CAPSIZE DRILLS

Canoes and kayaks capsize, or flip over. It is part of what makes the sport fun and exciting! All paddlers need to be prepared for the inevitable flip and know how to right the boat, drain any water it collects, and re-enter.

The best way to deal with a water-filled canoe is to put the paddle in the canoe and swim the boat to shore. Once on shore, tilt the canoe on its side to drain out all the water.

When a kayak capsizes, grab the paddle so it does not float away! Turn the kayak upright by lifting it up and flipping at the same time to drain water from the cockpit. Strap the paddle float onto the paddle blade and inflate it. Attach the opposite paddle blade onto the kayak with the bungees. This stabilizes the kayak. Put one foot on the paddle throat. Scramble onto the back deck facedown and slowly lower feet into the cockpit. Slowly turn over until sitting in the kayak.

Kayakers wearing spray skirts have the added option of doing an Eskimo roll to right their flipped kayak. This is an advanced skill that relies heavily upon flicking the hips and sweeping the paddle to get back into an upright position.

Being capsized in a kayak can be a scary experience, but with enough practice, getting out of a jam like this is no problem.

SAFETY

SAFETY GEAR

The most important piece of equipment when paddling is a life jacket. Paddlers call it a personal flotation device, or PFD for short.

The U.S. Coast Guard requires that life jackets be within reach, in good condition, and the appropriate size for every person on the boat. PFDs are designed for men, women, children, and dogs. They should fit snugly and be brightly colored to be spotted easily. A loud emergency whistle should be attached to every life jacket.

Every canoe or kayak needs to have a throw rope or towrope attached to the front of the boat. Towropes are used to tow the boat somewhere. A throw rope can be thrown to rescue somebody in the water or in a boat. Every kayaker should have a paddle float for self-rescue.

PRO TIPS AND TRICKS

Every time canoes and kayaks go out onto the water a few essential safety items should always be packed: a first aid kit, extra food like energy bars or trail mix, and extra water in case a trip lasts longer than planned. Pack a map of the areas to be explored.

When it comes to safety gear, wearing a life jacket is a must. A helmet is also something good to wear because it protects your head in the event you tip over.

White-water kayakers especially need to wear helmets because the rough waters they travel through have rocks hidden under the waves.

Every group of boaters should have one extra paddle and a bilge pump. A bilge pump is a hand pump that pumps out water from inside the boat.

White-water canoers and kayakers should always wear helmets.

It is not enough to just have the required safety equipment. Everybody must know how to use it. This essential equipment could save a life if used correctly.

COMMON HAZARDS

Canoeing and kayaking, like all sports, has hazards that must be navigated to have a safe, fun time.

Always check the weather report before leaving home. Paddling in sunny, clear weather is much more fun than in windy, rainy weather.

If caught in a thunderstorm while on the water, get to land immediately. Lightning can be deadly. Find shelter in a building, or in a group of trees that are all the same size. Another option is to sit on a blanket, sleeping pad, or dry bag with feet drawn as close to the body as possible. This will minimize the risk of being hit by lightning.

When the storm clouds come rolling in, it's time for the canoes to come out.

DID YOU KNOW?

Lip balm is always good to bring. Especially with wind, but also with cold and hot weather, blistering and peeling lips is likely, and that is never fun.

On hot days prevent overheating by dipping hands and arms in the water. Cool off with a wet cloth around the neck. Even better, take a break and go swimming! On cold days wear lots of layers to put on or take off as needed.

Wildlife is beautiful to watch but do not touch! Many animals bite or sting when they are scared. Wildlife does not benefit from human interaction, so keep a safe distance away from the animals.

When a larger boat passes by it creates a series of swells, or smooth looking waves also called wake. Point the front of the canoe or kayak toward the swells because a strong swell that hits a small boat on its side may capsize, or flip it over.

While seeing some of the wildlife in their natural habitat might be a pleasant sight, it's best to not get to too close and observe from a distance

READING A RIVER

Rivers, streams, lakes, and currents change every day. A trip down the same stretch of water will be different from one day to the next. Always look ahead and know what kind of water to expect.

Take note of objects in the water like rocks, bridges, and trees. Downstream from these objects is calm water called an eddy. These large objects are blocking the current and eddies are an excellent place to rest.

It is important to make sure the area that will be paddled along isn't out of your skill range.

Wind pushing from behind makes paddling fun and easy, but a headwind can make even an easy trip challenging, and exhausting. Listen to the weather report for the wind speed. Wind is commonly measured in knots.

While the decision to paddle depends upon skill level, currents, wind, and location it is not recommended to paddle in anything over 20 knots.

Paddlers need to understand water's natural movements. There are three types: tide, current, tidal current.

Wind (knots)	Description	Appearance of water
1-3	light air	ripples
4-6	light breeze	small wavelets
7-10	gentle breeze	large wavelets, crests begin to break
11-16	moderate breeze	small waves 1-4 feet, some whitecaps
17-21	fresh breeze	moderate waves 4-8 feet, many whitecaps, some spray
22-27	strong breeze	larger waves 8-13 feet, more spray

Rough waters can usually make a trip more fun, but only if the rider is capable of handling the current.

Tide is the predictable daily movement of the water up and down due to gravitational forces.

Current is the side-to-side movement of water. An example is a river after rain when there is more water and the current moves faster downstream.

Tidal current is a current that is caused by the tide and is useful when navigating small creeks or channels just off the ocean or a large lake.

Having a safety whistle is important because sometimes the unexpected can happen.

RESCUE

Make a safety or float plan for every trip. Write down where the boat will enter and exit the water, the route, planned stops, who is going, and the expected return time. Leave the float plan with a trustworthy adult. If the paddlers do not return on time, the float plan can be followed to rescue the lost or stranded paddlers.

When trying to communicate with someone far away use a paddle to signal. Some groups have their own signals but there are a few well-known signals to know.

OK: hold one arm out to the side and pat fingertips on top of head, forming an 'O' with the arm. This can be used as a question and as an answer.

Emergency: hold hand or paddle vertically above head and wave side to side quickly.

Stop: hold paddle horizontally over head.

Another way to get attention is with an emergency whistle. Three short blasts on a whistle means distress.

Paddlers that lose their boat or swimmers that can no longer swim need to be rescued and taken to shore. If they are close let them grab on to a paddle and pull them to the boat. If the swimmer is far away hold on to one end of the throw rope and toss the rest so that it lands behind them. Have them hold on to the side of the boat or onto the boat's bow and put their legs around the hull.

Although being involved in competitions is different, always canoeing or kayaking with a rope is important because it can still aid in your rescue.

CANOEING & KAYAKING ADVENTURES

RAPIDS

Paddlers who feel the need for speed go white-water paddling. It gets its name from the fast moving water. As it goes around, over, and through obstacles the water becomes so turbulent that the surface is broken and it looks white.

Water is designated Class 1-6 but changes frequently due to storms, seasonal rain, and snow melt. Before attempting to paddle rapids, speak to a knowledgeable guide or expert to find out the current water conditions. Never paddle above skill level. It is always better to carry the boat downriver to calmer water.

- **Class 1**: Easy to navigate and fairly smooth
- **Class 2**: Moderate maneuvering required, medium-quick water
- **Class 3**: Difficult with complex navigation required, large irregular waves; must be scouted before paddling
- **Class 4**: Very difficult and dangerous; rapids are powerful and precise navigation is necessary to handle intense, and dangerous currents; a strong Eskimo roll is highly recommended, canoes need special equipment to prevent swamping

PRO TIPS AND TRICKS

Most times, canoers and kayakers capsize unexpectedly. This is why it is important to wear your life jacket at all times. In the event of something happening like a wave, collision, or even wind, there might not be enough reaction time to put a jacket on.

Most accidents in the water occur when riders try to take on waters they aren't skilled enough to handle.

PRO TIPS AND TRICKS

As with all other outdoor sports, respect the wildlife and animals that live there. Observe from a safe distance and always leave everything where you find it.

- **Class 5**: Extremely difficult with large drops, holes, and dangerous rapids that cannot be avoided. Boats can easily be pinned and rescues are dangerous.
- **Class 6**: Extraordinarily dangerous and paddled by experts under the best conditions only because the risk of injury or death is likely and rescue may not be possible.

White-water paddlers wear helmets, whistles, and PFDs. They frequently practice self-rescues and how to rescue other paddlers.

CLUBS & COMPETITION

Many schools and communities have clubs for canoeing and kayaking paddlers. These groups get together to paddle, have fun, and learn from each other. Many clubs organize classes for their members to improve their skills and have member discounts at local paddling stores. They help at community events and are often called upon to be safety observers at open-water

Shown here is Long Beach Junior Crew as it races in the Head of Charles Regatta on October 20, 2013 in Boston, Massachusetts.

swimming competitions. Or they may participate in river clean-ups.

Races are held around the United States and the world. They have divisions for different age, sex, and skill levels that allow everybody to have fun paddling, make new friends, and get a chance to win a race.

Kayakers have a crazy race called 8 Ball, which is their version of NASCAR. Multiple kayakers take off on a 200-meter white-water race at the same time. As they navigate the rapids, rocks, and other racers they

A Canadian kayaker is shown competing during the 2008 Olympic team trials at the U.S. National Whitewater Center for the Whitewater Slalom event in Charlotte, North Carolina.

A canoer is shown at the start of the Open Canoe Whitewater Slalom Race on Gull River.

have to watch out for the 8 ballers. 8 ballers are non-racing kayakers wearing body armor that are waiting downriver. Their sole purpose is to do everything they can to hit, block, create chaos, and slow down the racers.

Canoeing and kayaking are Summer Olympics sports for both men and women. Canoeing and kayaking have been featured as competition sports in the Summer Olympic Games since the 1936 Games, although they were demonstration sports at the 1924 Games in Paris. There are two divisions: slalom and sprint. Slalom is a course requiring paddlers to maneuver through rapids as fast as possible. Sprint is a race in a straight line for speed. Sprint races vary from 200-meter to 1,000-meter races for solo, tandem, and four-person team paddlers.

FAMOUS PEOPLE

The most famous paddler is kayaker Tao Berman. He holds three world records, including the world record waterfall descent. He fell 98.4 feet at Johnston Falls in Alberta, Canada and reached about 55 miles per hour during his fall! Tao is the first person to complete over fifty waterfall descents around the world.

Tao is thirty-four years old and has been kayaking since he was fourteen. He is an expert and has never been seriously injured. Part of that is due to the fact that he practices five days a week and has a rigorous workout schedule. Tao does 1,200 pull-ups a week, runs up 1,260 stairs a week, and paddles a Class 5 rapid five days a week! He has made a career out of kayaking and makes over $250,000 a year.

Over his Summer Break in 2012 Benton Purnell, a seventeen-year-old, canoed all 2,350 miles of the Mississippi River in sixty-seven days. During his trip Benton saw a wolf, had a fish jump into his canoe, was charged by a beaver, and attacked by a duck.

In 2011 a sixty-four-year-old Polish man named Aleksander Doba crossed the Atlantic Ocean in a sea kayak. It took him ninety-nine days to travel over 3,300 miles from Senegal, on the West Coast of Africa, to Brazil in South America. His sea kayak was 23 feet long but only 39 inches wide.

DID YOU KNOW?

White-water paddlers carry throw ropes, flares, and rescue knives because it can be a very dangerous sport.

When planning a canoe or kayak adventure, make sure to give sufficient time. You might not want to leave.

PLAN YOUR OWN ADVENTURE

Plan and ensure a safe, fun trip. Read guidebooks to find out the hazards and water classification. Talk to local experts about the route. Find out the current water conditions and the weather forecast.

Expect the unexpected. Pack emergency gear that will get all paddlers through a worst-case scenario.

Before every trip make and check a list to be sure everything is packed.

When planning a trip consider these questions. "Yes" should be the answer.

- Is the route and water within the skill level of all paddlers?

- Do all paddlers have the strength and endurance for the trip?

- If a paddler flips, do they have the skill and knowledge to self-rescue? If not, will another paddler be able to safely help rescue them?

- Is there a paddle plan detailing the trip left with somebody not going on the trip?

- Will the weather be appropriate for paddling?

- Do all the paddlers have a correctly fitting PFD?

- Is the emergency equipment packed: first aid kit, energy bars, extra water, map?

Whether a lazy river ride or a heart-pounding white-water rapid, paddling is a fun sport for all ages and skill levels. Enjoy the great outdoors with a local club, a friend, or family member and get paddling!

FURTHER READING

BOOKS

De Medeiros, James. *Kayaking*. New York: Weigl, 2013.

Hardyman, Robyn. *Kayaking and Canoeing*. New York: Windmill Books, 2013.

Mattos, Bill. *Kayaking & Canoeing for Beginners*. Leicester, UK: Anness Publishing LTD., 2004.

McGuffin, Gary. *Paddle Your Own Canoe: An Illustrated Guide to the Art of Canoeing*. Ontario: Firefly Books, 2003.

Molloy, Johnny. *Outward Bound Canoeing Handbook*. Guilford, CT: FalconGuides, 2014.

Stuhaug, Dennis. *Kayaking Made Easy: A Manual for Beginners with Tips for the Experienced*. Guilford, Conn.: FalconGuides, 2006.

INTERNET ADDRESSES

About.com Kayak and Canoe Site
<http://paddling.about.com/>

ACA (American Canoe Association)
<http://www.americancanoe.org/>

KayakGuide.com
<http://www.kayakguide.com/>

The Ultimate Guide to Canoeing, Paddlesports, Canoeing Gear, and Canoeing Destinations
<http://www.canoeing.com/>

INDEX